# JOURNEY TO THE
# SECRET PLACE

## JEFF STRUSS

|FOREWORD BY: PATRICIA BOOTSMA|

### 30 DAY DEVOTIONAL

*Elani*
PUBLISHING

For information contact :
http://www.elanipublishing.com

Cover design and interior layout by Peter Mitchell
ISBN: 978-0-578-62744-1

First Edition: January 2020

# FOREWORD BY PATRICIA BOOTSMA

When I first met Jeff Struss, it was easy to discern he was a man of deep abiding connection with the Lord. There is something about a person who has cultivated a history in God where their spirit man matures to radiate an atmosphere of the Presence all around them. That was the case for the 17th-century monk known as Brother Lawrence who so oozed the Holy Spirit, people would come from afar to simply watch him wash dishes or peel carrots. Now, in these last days, the Lord is raising up many of the nameless and faceless who will so carry the Glory of the Lord they will help shift atmospheres, start revival fires and bring societal reformation.

Isaiah 60 reminds us the Glory (in Hebrew chabod) will arise over us and radiate through us even though deep darkness may cover the earth. The next chapter, Isaiah 61, reveals that Glory anoints us, like Jesus, to 'preach good tidings to the poor...heal the brokenhearted, proclaim liberty to the captives... open the prison to those who are bound... proclaim the acceptable year of the Lord...". The billion-soul harvest prophesied will come in and Jesus will split the sky and come again. We can be a part of all of this, we can be ready. How? Jeff helps uncover the key - abide in the Presence of the Lord in the Secret Place.

Here we cultivate a heart of tender love, here we exercise the Great Commandment (Matthew 22:37- 40), here we are empowered for the Great Commission (Matthew 28:18-20), here we buy oil so when the bridegroom comes, we are welcomed into that wedding feast (Matthew 25:1-13). There is nothing so worthwhile and of such eternal significance as cultivating a heart of love. May this be the greatest pursuit of our lives. Jeff Struss' wonderful devotional, Journey to the Secret Place, will help us in this epic goal.

Patricia Bootsma
Pastoral Leader - Catch the Fire Canada and Catch the Fire U.S.A.
Author - Convergence: Keys to Destiny; Raising Burning Hearts: Parenting and Mentoring Next Generation Lovers of God and A Lifestyle of Divine Encounters: Through Prayer, Prophesy and the Power of the Living Word

# INTRODUCTION

I wrote this devotional because I love helping people step into a deeper place in experience of the Presence of God.

When God took hold of my life, I was a broken, addicted, and bound young man. At 18 years of age I was lost and depressed and my brokenness led me to pick up a Bible to see what answers it might have for me.

In the back of a public high school library, I opened the Bible and began reading the book of Proverbs.

It was there that God broke into my life.

His Presence began washing over me and my life was changed. I wept in repentance in that place and my love for His Presence began that same day.

I would often go home after school or after work and shut the door to my bedroom and sit on the floor, laying the Bible out before me.

I would say, "God, would you come and visit me. I want to know you."

And you know what? He did. Time after time.

His Presence would invade my bedroom and He began changing my life.

It was during those times that I found the path to the Secret Place.

The Secret Place is the place of encounter. It is the place of prayer. It is the place of communion, and it is the place of intimacy. It is the place of revelation and it is the place of empowerment. It is the place of identity, destiny, calling and gifting. It is the place of transformation but most of all, it is the place of knowing Him.

And that, "knowing Him," that is our greatest prize.

But how do we move into a place of heart to heart and face to face communion?

There is no prescription or magic words. But I have found some principles to be true.

## 1. SET ASIDE TIME AND SPACE

How much time? Start with what you have. Go deep with what you have and let your heart grow and expand. Know this: He will fill however many vessels you give Him!

## 2. START WITH WORSHIP. START WITH HIS WORD

Don't start with your feelings. Start with Him. Start with His feelings. Declare who He is. Thank Him for Who He is and what He has done. Let the truth of God's Word begin to change your heart and mind afresh.

## 3. ADORE HIM

This is personal. This is private. Pour your love on Him. Tell Him how beautiful He is. Worship Him some more. Use your words. He loves your voice. Draw near to Him and tell Him that you desire to draw near. Invite Him afresh to touch you and touch your life.

## 4. BE STILL

Stop talking. Be still. Face to face. Heart to heart. Union.

## 5. REPEAT :-)

Again, this is not a "magic formula" that will get you what you want. These are merely "sign posts" that may very well be helpful for you to step into a new level of prayer and intimacy with Christ.

The devotionals found in this book draw on the principles above. Each devotional is based upon a scripture or a passage that I have used to draw near to Christ. Scripture is truth and our encounters with Christ must be based on the truth for He Himself is the Truth.

So anchor your heart and mind in God's word and let the Holy Spirit breath on you as you read His Word and let fresh love for Jesus rise up in your heart.

I've added space for journaling each day.
Journaling is amazing because you can reflect on how you prayed, what you prayed, how God has answered your prayers, and how you have changed over time.

Feel free to write your prayers to the Lord and interact with the text however

you like.

The journey into the heart of God is for the adventurous. Scripture says, "It is the glory of God to conceal a matter, but the glory of kings is to search out a matter." There is a glory that God has reserved for you and I as His kings and priests. It is the glory of seeking Him out in greater and greater depths.

The simple fact that you are reading this right now is proof and evidence that the Father is drawing you to Himself... You are already on your way!

My prayer is that you would fall deeper and deeper into the love of God. That passion and desire for Jesus would grow and blossom and bloom into maturity into your heart. That God might use this book as fuel for the fire and a provocation for pressing in.

He loves you.

Let's press in to know Him more,

Jeff Struss
2019

# DAY 1

"AS THE DEER PANTS FOR THE WATER BROOKS, SO PANTS MY SOUL FOR YOU, O GOD.
MY SOUL THIRSTS FOR GOD, FOR THE LIVING GOD.
WHEN SHALL I COME AND APPEAR BEFORE GOD?"
| PSALM 42:1-2 |

---

Deep within the heart of humanity is the cry... It's the cry of the ancients and it's the cry of you and I today: When shall I come and appear before God?

Its moving past the place of story and past the place of teaching. It pushes through the noise and the discouragement and the cynicism and it makes it's appeal to dead religion, "There must be more than this!"

It's the cry of the humble. It's the cry of the hungry. It's the cry of the seeker who longs for the Bread of His Presence, and it's the cry of the satisfied who has tasted and yet longs for it more and more.

It's the cry of your heart that drew you to this book. It's the cry of your heart that burns for more of your Savior and your King.

It's the cry of the thirsty who won't be satisfied with second hand information... No. This cry can not be satisfied with another man's encounter. I must encounter God myself!

When can I come and appear before God?!?

And when this cry goes up, and when we look to Him again, and when we realize that He has come to us, we realize we've made it home.

Our hearts are warming now to His Presence. He is all around us, inside of us, over us, beneath us. He is a shield round about us... And we realize... We are there. We are home. We are in the Secret Place of His Presence.

NOW SET THE ATTENTION OF YOUR HEART ON THE LORD.
RECEIVE THE LOVE OF JESUS
AND LOVE HIM IN RETURN.

_____
_____
_____
_____
_____
_____
_____
_____
_____
_____
_____
_____
_____
_____
_____
_____
_____
_____
_____
_____
_____
_____
_____
_____
_____
_____

# JOURNAL

# DAY 2

"HE WHO DWELLS IN THE SECRET PLACE OF THE MOST HIGH SHALL ABIDE UNDER THE SHADOW OF THE ALMIGHTY."
| PSALM 91:1 |

---

Because there is a secret place... There is a hiding place. There is a tower that we can run into and we are saved. It is the place of our God. It is the place of protection. It is the place of deliverance. It is the salvation of our God.

We look to Him... We gaze at Him... We push past the attack of the enemy and the oppression of our days and we touch eternity and eternity responds to us.

It is the place where demonic schemes come to nothing.

It is the place where sickness and disease can't stand to go.

It is the place where fear and worry and anxiety disappears for we were made for eternity and eternity is touching us right here... right now.

Even right now. I close my eyes and realize... He's here. All around me.

Right now I enter into the realm of my Father. I'm safe. I'm secure. I've arrived at my destination.

It's a hidden place... A place that's reserved... Room for one. One at a time anyways. A secret place. An intimate place. Secret from the eyes of men... but more!

Secret from the demonic realms of the enemy of our soul. He can't find us here. It's a secret place and a hidden place and here I enter into a no fly zone of the spirits of darkness of the air.

Here it is spirit to spirit and face to face. Here I run and here I am saved.

Today I step in. Today I touch heaven. Even now as I turn the affections of my heart toward my God, He comes to me and it is here that I will dwell.

NOW SET THE ATTENTION OF YOUR HEART ON THE LORD.
RECEIVE THE LOVE OF JESUS
AND LOVE HIM IN RETURN.

_____
_____
_____
_____
_____
_____
_____
_____
_____
_____
_____
_____
_____
_____
_____
_____
_____
_____
_____
_____
_____
_____
_____
_____
_____
_____
_____
_____
_____
_____
_____

# JOURNAL

# DAY 3

"LORD, YOU HAVE BEEN OUR DWELLING PLACE IN ALL GENERATIONS."
| PSALM 90:1 |

Where is home? Where can I find my place of rest? Where can I turn to and where can I run?

Is it a location that I can travel to? O that I might know the way! Surely if I could travel there I would sell all just to live in that place... The place of protection, the place of security. The place of provision and the place of peace.

Yes. I would sell all and pay any price to travel there and live in that place.

And yet that place does not exist on earth as we know it. There must be a place! Yes, there must be!

What about God? What about Him? What about His presence? What about His person? Could I dwell there? Could I live "there"... "In Him"? O that I could experience that peace that passes understanding! O that I could enter into eternity... right now! To step into that place of "abiding" that I would "remain" in Him.

So I will. Yes, I must! I must press past the noise and the confusion and the pain.... Yes I will press on! I will step into His presence again! But... to leave? Must I leave? Must I leave Him here? In this room? Must I walk out only to long to return again?

Can't there be more?!

Yes, there is. I will make HIM my dwelling place. Yes I will live In Him. I will hide in Him. I will make my residence In Him. I will dwell In Him. Communion. Intimacy.

An exchange of life for life. All of me, for all of Him. All of Him, consuming all of me. To step into life. To remain. To dwell. This is my Secret Place.

NOW SET THE ATTENTION OF YOUR HEART ON THE LORD.
RECEIVE THE LOVE OF JESUS
AND LOVE HIM IN RETURN.

_____
_____
_____
_____
_____
_____
_____
_____
_____
_____
_____
_____
_____
_____
_____
_____
_____
_____
_____
_____
_____
_____
_____

# JOURNAL

# DAY 4

"ONE THING I HAVE DESIRED OF THE LORD, THAT WILL I SEEK: THAT I MAY DWELL IN THE HOUSE OF THE LORD ALL THE DAYS OF MY LIFE, TO BEHOLD THE BEAUTY OF THE LORD, AND TO INQUIRE IN HIS TEMPLE. FOR IN THE TIME OF TROUBLE HE SHALL HIDE ME IN HIS PAVILION: IN THE SECRET PLACE OF HIS TABERNACLE HE SHALL HIDE ME: HE SHALL SET ME HIGH UPON A ROCK."

| PSALM 27:4-5 |

---

Where are you? Where are you now? What troubles you? What concerns you? What threatens you? What has your attention? What has your gaze?

David was pursued. He was hunted. Not by irrational fears or anxieties, but by an army. By angry men with weapons, who, if they found him would kill him.

But David found a place... no one knew about it. Not even the mad king and the enraged army. No earthly man knew about this place, but neither did the enemy of his soul. No demon, no devil, no principality knew about this place.

It was, "The Secret Place."

It was (and is) the place that appears. You could go in right now. In fact you should.

Yes. Walk in right now. It's the place of protection. It's the place of peace. It's the place of heaven breaking into everything that is wrong with us.

His Presence comes and we... are... SAFE.

"Where is the door?" you ask. You know The Way and you have the key.

The Way is the God-Man Christ Jesus.
The key is "one thing". To gaze. To worship. To adore.
Yes. Use that key! Walk down the way! Worship your God!
The Secret Place awaits.

NOW SET THE ATTENTION OF YOUR HEART ON THE LORD.
RECEIVE THE LOVE OF JESUS
AND LOVE HIM IN RETURN.

_____
_____
_____
_____
_____
_____
_____
_____
_____
_____
_____
_____
_____
_____
_____
_____
_____
_____
_____
_____
_____
_____
_____
_____
_____
_____
_____
_____

# JOURNAL

# DAY 5

**"THEN (MOSES) SAID TO HIM, 'IF YOUR PRESENCE DOES NOT GO WITH US, DO NOT BRING US UP FROM HERE.'"**
| EXODUS 33:15 |

---

Can a man argue with God?

Can the created bring a complaint against the Creator?

In no way and in no sense can we become His advisor.
In no way and in no sense can we correct Him.

But as a friend...

As a friend we come before Him. As a worshipper, as a follower as one who is sold out and committed... even a slave for Love's sake.

Are you content without Him?

Will you go on without Him?

Will you pick up what you have and leave without first touching heaven?

Oh that we would have a heart that says, "If Your Presence does not go with us, do not bring us up from here!" For this is the cry of a lover. This is the cry of the devoted. This is not the cry of the natural man or the "religious" man or the easily satisfied.

It is the cry of the hungry and it is the desire of the thirsty.

Don't you want His Presence? Don't you want His Presence? For His Presence is His person and in Him we find everything.

He is our everything. And today... right now... in this moment... we step in. Oh that we would see His Glory.

NOW SET THE ATTENTION OF YOUR HEART ON THE LORD.
RECEIVE THE LOVE OF JESUS
AND LOVE HIM IN RETURN.

_____
_____
_____
_____
_____
_____
_____
_____
_____
_____
_____
_____
_____
_____
_____
_____
_____
_____
_____
_____
_____
_____
_____
_____
_____
_____
_____
_____
_____
_____
_____
_____

# JOURNAL

# DAY 6

"AND (MOSES) SAID, 'PLEASE, SHOW ME YOUR GLORY.' THEN HE SAID, "I WILL MAKE ALL MY GOODNESS PASS BEFORE YOU, AND I WILL PROCLAIM THE NAME OF THE LORD BEFORE YOU.'"
| EXODUS 33:18-19 |

---

Yes God! If we have found favor in your sight... If you have loved us... If you have chosen us... If you have died for us, and have been raised for us. If you have heard us, and you see us. If you have called us to Yourself.

Then God, O God, draw me to Yourself. I want to see your face! I want to see Your glory!

Not only Your ways, O God. Yes, Your ways... But O, to see the face of God.

To walk where Adam walked. To dwell where Christ now dwells. I want to experience your love O God like never before.

Past the crowds.
Past the routines.
Past the motions.
Through the stories and within a Secret Place... there... God... dwells.


In all His glory.
His goodness.
His beauty.
His splendor.

That I would know the name of God.

Holy.
Righteous.
Clean.
Pure.
Show me Your face O God. Please show me Your Glory.

NOW SET THE ATTENTION OF YOUR HEART ON THE LORD.
RECEIVE THE LOVE OF JESUS
AND LOVE HIM IN RETURN.

_____
_____
_____
_____
_____
_____
_____
_____
_____
_____
_____
_____
_____
_____
_____
_____
_____
_____
_____
_____
_____
_____
_____
_____
_____
_____
_____
_____
_____
_____

# JOURNAL

# DAY 7

**"AND THE LORD SAID, 'SHALL I HIDE FROM ABRAHAM WHAT I AM DOING?'"**
| GENESIS 18:17 |

---

Lord God... my God.

You said in your word that Abraham was your friend.
How does a man become a friend of God?
How does a man with weakness and sin capture the heart of a holy and
exalted God?

Lord your told your disciples that you called them friends... because you told
them what you were doing.

And there is a place of friendship that is open. Here... right now. In the place of
communion and the place of the burning heart.

God speaks to man. And God speaks to me!

O God! That I would be your friend! Help my heart respond to Love in such a
way that I would be close to your heart... leaning on your heart... relying on
your heart... FAITHFUL with your heart... the very heart of God.

Beating.
Pulsing.
Driving.
His heart beats for me now and I enter in again.
Communion.
Intimacy.
Friendship.

Face to face and heart to heart.

And as I enter in I hear the voice of the Father speaking to me... mysteries...
secrets... the deep things of God.

Past acquaintance and into friendship. I enter in today. Humbly, I am Yours.

NOW SET THE ATTENTION OF YOUR HEART ON THE LORD.
RECEIVE THE LOVE OF JESUS
AND LOVE HIM IN RETURN.

_____
_____
_____
_____
_____
_____
_____
_____
_____
_____
_____
_____
_____
_____
_____
_____
_____
_____
_____
_____
_____
_____
_____
_____
_____
_____

# JOURNAL

# DAY 8

**"AND GOD SAID, 'LET US MAKE MAN IN OUR IMAGE, ACCORDING TO OUR LIKENESS.'"**
| GENESIS 1:26 |

---

God I can feel you now. You are not distant and far off. You are here! You are making me and molding me and changing me.

Something is happening. Something hidden. Something deep. Something that has not yet been revealed.

For you are forming me and making me and shaping me in a Secret Place.

In the Secret Place of your Presence you are forming yourself in me.

For its always been your desire.
Its always been your aim. That the fullness of the Trinity would dwell in human form.

That in Christ you have called me into union with the Trinity... Union with Christ... Union with the Godhead.

And I bring nothing to the table.
And I add nothing to the process.
I am and remain dependent.

Totally.
Fully.
Wholly dependent on Perfect Love being formed in me.

And you draw me to Yourself again. And you shape me to Yourself again.
And I step into the flaming furnace of perfect Love.

I am changed here. This secret place is a transformation of Love.
God is being formed in me. Here. Now. Today.

I embrace the Flame.

NOW SET THE ATTENTION OF YOUR HEART ON THE LORD.
RECEIVE THE LOVE OF JESUS
AND LOVE HIM IN RETURN.

_____
_____
_____
_____
_____
_____
_____
_____
_____
_____
_____
_____
_____
_____
_____
_____
_____
_____
_____
_____
_____
_____
_____
_____
_____
_____
_____
_____
_____

# JOURNAL

# DAY 9

"THEN (JACOB) DREAMED, AND BEHOLD, A LADDER WAS SET UP ON THE EARTH, AND ITS TOP REACHED TO HEAVEN; AND THERE THE ANGELS OF GOD WERE ASCENDING AND DESCENDING ON IT.'"
| GENESIS 28:12 |

---

Lord God, where can I go where Heaven touches the earth?

Jacob came to you in a lonely place... a dry place... a wilderness place. He took a rock from the ground and laid his head upon it. It became a secret place for Jacob and he met with God there.

And God appeared!
And the heavens were open!
His secret place became a place of encounter, and promise, and destiny and intimacy.

Where the God of his fathers and the God of his past became his God and his future.

It's the place of encounter and it's the place of revelation. For we are not alone!
We are not fighting on our own.
For you have ordained strength for us.
You have ordained help.
Have you not said that you have appointed angels to minister to your people?
Have you not said that your angels as flames of fire and messengers riding on the winds?

God of my future. God of my past. God of my today. Open to me the treasures of an open heaven.

Give unto me the treasure of your revelation. Give unto me the treasure of communion and intimacy today. Give unto me the blessing of knowing You... Are... With Me.
Your angels surround me now. Heaven is here. Help is Here. Future is Here.
The door is open now... so I walk in.

NOW SET THE ATTENTION OF YOUR HEART ON THE LORD.
RECEIVE THE LOVE OF JESUS
AND LOVE HIM IN RETURN.

_____
_____
_____
_____
_____
_____
_____
_____
_____
_____
_____
_____
_____
_____
_____
_____
_____
_____
_____
_____
_____
_____
_____
_____
_____
_____
_____
_____

# JOURNAL

# DAY 10

"SO THE LORD SPOKE TO MOSES FACE TO FACE, AS A MAN SPEAKS TO HIS FRIEND. AND HE WOULD RETURN TO THE CAMP, BUT HIS SERVANT JOSHUA THE SON OF NUN, A YOUNG MAN, DID NOT DEPART FROM THE TABERNACLE."
| EXODUS 33:11 |

---

So you would meet with Moses and Joshua in a secret place... a tent... a tabernacle. A normal place became a Holy Place because you showed Yourself there.
You revealed Yourself in that place. It was the place of Your Presence. It was the place of your Person. It was the place of The Face.

And so they came to meet with you. And so You would come and meet with them. Face to Face. Heart to heart. God would meet with man.

Time would pass... much time. Minutes. Hours.
Eventually Moses would leave.
But Joshua...

Selah

Joshua would remain in the tent.
Joshua would remain fixed on Your Glory. Fixed on Your Presence.
Joshua entered in a little longer. Gazed a little deeper.

He would worship and he would weep.
He would pray and he would listen.
He would wonder and he would receive.

Wave after wave. Billow after billow. You would come to that place.
Today you come to me.
I have a heart like Joshua O God. To stay. To remain. To abide. To see a little more and lay hold of something beyond. This is our Secret Place O God.
All of me, for all of You. My time, my energy, my focus, my attention. I give it all.
You... Are... So... Beautiful.

NOW SET THE ATTENTION OF YOUR HEART ON THE LORD.
RECEIVE THE LOVE OF JESUS
AND LOVE HIM IN RETURN.

_____
_____
_____
_____
_____
_____
_____
_____
_____
_____
_____
_____
_____
_____
_____
_____
_____
_____
_____
_____
_____
_____
_____
_____
_____

# JOURNAL

# DAY 11

"...I SAW THE LORD SITTING ON A THRONE, HIGH AND LIFTED UP, AND THE TRAIN OF HIS ROBE FILLED THE TEMPLE. ABOVE IT STOOD SERAPHIM... AND ONE CRIED TO ANOTHER AND SAID: HOLY, HOLY, HOLY IS THE LORD OF HOSTS; THE WHOLE EARTH IS FULL OF HIS GLORY!' AND THE POSTS OF THE DOOR WERE SHAKEN BY THE VOICE OF HIM WHO CRIED OUT, AND THE HOUSE WAS FILLED WITH SMOKE"
| ISAIAH 6:1-4 |

---

And I can see you now... There You are... King of Glory. High and lifted up. Magnificent. Radiant. Wonderful. Beautiful. Awesome in splendor. There is no one like you.

There you are Holy. Perfect. Majestic in wonder and wholly and completely your own. There is truly no one like you.

You stand alone. You are the Lily of the Valley and one among ten thousand. I could give everything I have for this love and it would be despised.

Yet you call me. You beckon me. The smoke of your glory fills the room now. Your Presence is calling me deeper. Deeper than I've ever been before.

Deeper than what I am comfortable with and deeper than what I think I deserve.

For you have place your love upon me. You have joined yourself to me.

I stand with the angels now. Yes. I worship.

I stand with the angels and I cry the cry of eternity:

Holy. Holy. Holy.
I lift my voice. I lift my heart. I enter in.

NOW SET THE ATTENTION OF YOUR HEART ON THE LORD.
RECEIVE THE LOVE OF JESUS
AND LOVE HIM IN RETURN.

_____
_____
_____
_____
_____
_____
_____
_____
_____
_____
_____
_____
_____
_____
_____
_____
_____
_____
_____
_____
_____
_____
_____
_____
_____
_____
_____
_____

# JOURNAL

# DAY 12

"...HEAVEN IS MY THRONE, AND EARTH IS MY FOOTSTOOL. WHERE IS THE HOUSE THAT YOU WILL BUILD ME? AND WHERE IS THE PLACE OF MY REST?...BUT ON THIS ONE WILL I LOOK: ON HIM WHO IS POOR AND OF A CONTRITE SPRIT, AND WHO TREMBLES AT MY WORD."
| ISAIAH 66:1-2 |

---

God... Almighty God... Maker of Heaven and earth. He desires a resting place. He desires a home.

What can you build for God? What stones or jewels or metals could you use that would impress Him?

How big would the structure need to be... to house God?

Regardless of the amount of time, or the amount of money spent... Regardless of the size or the intricacy of the structure... How could it impress God? And what possibly be fitting for Him?

Yet God desires a home.
God desires a resting place.
He looks for a home that is appropriate for Him.

And now... He looks... to you.

You are His choice. You are His home.
God in all His splendor and all His majesty has decided to come and make His home in you.
He isn't compromising. He isn't settling. He is happy to dwell there. He has longed to dwell there.
To dwell with the humble. To dwell with the hungry. To dwell with those who love His Word and love His ways.

You have always been His choice. His Presence coming and resting... staying... abiding... dwelling in you. Not for a moment. For all of eternity. He has chosen to dwell in you.
You are in Him. He is in you. Wrapped up and covered in divine love you realize the separation has vanished.
God has taken residence in you.

NOW SET THE ATTENTION OF YOUR HEART ON THE LORD.
RECEIVE THE LOVE OF JESUS
AND LOVE HIM IN RETURN.

_____
_____
_____
_____
_____
_____
_____
_____
_____
_____
_____
_____
_____
_____
_____
_____
_____
_____
_____
_____
_____
_____
_____
_____
_____

# JOURNAL

# DAY 13

"SO LET US KNOW, LET US PRESS ON TO KNOW THE LORD. HIS GOING FORTH IS AS CERTAIN
AS THE DAWN; AND HE WILL COME TO US LIKE THE RAIN, LIKE THE SPRING RAIN WATERING
THE EARTH"
| HOSEA 6:3 NASB |

---

The prophet calls to you and to me: press on, press in. Yes! Press into God, your God. Your Father and your King. Your Savior and the Lover of your soul. He is your God and He is calling you to Himself today.

He will come to you. He will make His face to shine upon you. Even as the sun rises in the earth and brings with it light and heat and new possibilities wrapped up in a fresh morning; so God, your God is rising upon you today.

He comes with His light. He comes with His rain. The light of His Presence warms and comforts.

His rain comes to refresh, renew, and restore.

Even now the rain of His Presence is falling on your heart. It is falling on the words that He has spoken to you. Every word of destiny, identity and calling have been residing in your soul like seeds in the earth.

The rain of His Presence comes, and the seeds begin to sprout.

Can't you see it?! The Lord your God is coming to you now! He has decided to shower you with His goodness and to cover you with His kindness! It is His good pleasure to visit you and draw you.

He has called you to Himself. Respond beloved! Press in! Lift the attention of your thoughts and mind to Him again!

He is calling you! It's you He desires and it's you He wants!

Respond and press in. Even now... fix your gaze upon His face. Let your heart be warmed by His Presence.
In this place... You. Are. Changed.

NOW SET THE ATTENTION OF YOUR HEART ON THE LORD.
RECEIVE THE LOVE OF JESUS
AND LOVE HIM IN RETURN.

_____

_____

_____

_____

_____

_____

_____

_____

_____

_____

_____

_____

_____

_____

_____

_____

_____

_____

_____

_____

_____

_____

_____

_____

_____

_____

_____

_____

_____

# JOURNAL

# DAY 14

"HE BOWED THE HEAVENS ALSO, AND CAME DOWN WITH DARKNESS UNDER HIS FEET. AND HE RODE UPON A CHERUB, AND FLEW; HE FLEW UPON THE WINGS OF THE WIND. HE MADE DARKNESS HIS SECRET PLACE..."
| PSALM 18:9-11 |

---

And the Lord bends down. He bends down from a high and lofty place and draws near... to you.

Angels all around you for angels are all around Him. All the atmosphere of heaven is filling your soul now as your God and your Creator beckons you to the Secret Place of His Presence.

It's a place of darkness and a place of mystery. It's the place of potential as the Spirit of God hovers and swarms around your very soul.

It's the same darkness that covered the earth at the dawn of creation. It's a hiddenness of what is about to break forth. And God is covering you and God is hiding you.

He is hiding you now in the Secret Place of His Presence and is forming you and making you into what He has always had in mind for you.

So God draws near. So God bends down. He is bringing heaven with Him! He has come with love. He has come with wind. He has come with angelic assistance.

He has come to draw you away, to conceal you and to protect you in a hidden place.

He is beckoning to you! Respond to Him! Love Him! Worship Him! Adore Him!

Worship Him until words fail to express what you feel. When you pass through to that place of stillness, darkness and mystery. Be still.

NOW SET THE ATTENTION OF YOUR HEART ON THE LORD.
RECEIVE THE LOVE OF JESUS
AND LOVE HIM IN RETURN.

_____
_____
_____
_____
_____
_____
_____
_____
_____
_____
_____
_____
_____
_____
_____
_____
_____
_____
_____
_____
_____
_____
_____
_____
_____
_____

# JOURNAL

# DAY 15

"O MY DOVE, IN THE CLEFTS OF THE ROCK, IN THE SECRET PLACES OF THE CLIFF, LET ME SEE YOUR FACE, LET ME HEAR YOUR VOICE; FOR YOUR VOICE IS SWEET, AND YOUR FACE IS LOVELY."
| SONG OF SOLOMON 2:14 |

---

Can you hear Him? He calls to you! Our Bridegroom, the Lover of your soul calls to you today!

He wants to see your face!

He wants to hear your voice!

He desires to see you, to know you, to be with you. He desires to be close to you!
Give Him a gift! Please respond and love Him in return!

What gift could you give?
Give Him the gift of your face.
Give Him the gift of your voice.

You don't think that is a gift?
It is a gift to Him for He has said:
Your voice is sweet!
Your face is lovely!

You move Him beloved! You have captured His heart! You have captured His gaze.
Tell Him you love Him! Use your voice. He loves your voice.
Lift your gaze to Him. Let Him see your face. He loves your face.

You have captured the heart of God and He longs to come away with you in the Secret Place. He longs to be with you there. He longs to hear from you there. He longs to gaze upon you there.
Give Him the gift of yourself. Love Him. Adore Him. He longs for you.

NOW SET THE ATTENTION OF YOUR HEART ON THE LORD.
RECEIVE THE LOVE OF JESUS
AND LOVE HIM IN RETURN.

_____
_____
_____
_____
_____
_____
_____
_____
_____
_____
_____
_____
_____
_____
_____
_____
_____
_____
_____
_____
_____
_____
_____
_____
_____
_____
_____
_____

# JOURNAL

# DAY 16

"BUT YOU, WHEN YOU PRAY, GO INTO YOUR ROOM, AND WHEN YOU HAVE SHUT YOUR DOOR, PRAY TO YOUR FATHER WHO IS IN THE SECRET PLACE; AND YOUR FATHER WHO SEES IN SECRET WILL REWARD YOU OPENLY"
| MATTHEW 6:6 |

---

Your Savior calls to you today. He calls for you to go.
Go. Rush. Run. Press through distractions and get to that place. The place where your Father is. The place where it's you and Him alone.

Are you alone? Are you there? Have you shut your door?

Some things shouldn't be shared with everyone. Some things are private. Some things are special. Some things are only for you and Him. Some things are treasured.

Your prayers. Your attention. Your adoration. Your fellowship. Your communion...This is what the Father desires. These are His treasures.

Right now, in this Secret Place of His Presence, God is coming to you. You have His attention, you have His heart.
Many men seek the praise of other men. Many men seek the attention of other men. Many men seek the company of other men.

But you... You have sought the attention of the Creator. You have sought the attention of your Maker. You have sought the company of God Almighty. And you have His heart.

Now speak. Pray. Pour out your love and affection to Him. He is listening now... He has promised to listen. He has promised to listen and He has promised to reward. Oh yes! There is a great reward. You exchange love for love in private, yet He is preparing rewards to give you in front of all.

Awesome God. Awesome Savior. Awesome power being released into your life. You are buying gold in the Secret Place of His Presence.

NOW SET THE ATTENTION OF YOUR HEART ON THE LORD.
RECEIVE THE LOVE OF JESUS
AND LOVE HIM IN RETURN.

# JOURNAL

# DAY 17

"AND HE WENT UP ON THE MOUNTAIN AND CALLED TO HIM THOSE HE HIMSELF WANTED.
AND THEY CAME TO HIM."
| MARK 3:13 |

---

Can you see Him? Can you hear Him? Ignore the crowd. Ignore the noise.
There He is! The Savior! The Teacher! There He is! He has been up all night
with His God and Your God. Now He is coming back. He speaks!

Did you hear it? Surely you must have heard it! He said your name! No, I am not
confused, He did. Listen...

There! You must have heard it that time. He said your name friend. He chose
you. He is calling you to Himself.
He is choosing YOU. He wants YOU. He desires YOU.

He wants you... To. Be. With. Him.

He wants you near Him. That's all. That's what He wants. He wants to be near
you and He wants you to be near to Him.

Won't you go to Him! Won't you respond! Ignore the crowd... push through.
Please push through the crowd! Don't let the crowd keep you from Him today.
He is worth the struggle. He is worth the effort. He is worth the time.

The crowd is mocking you?

Ignore them! Focus on the Teacher! He calls you to Himself. He calls for YOU
beloved. Look! He called others too. They are coming to Him. There are other
hungry hearts. There are other love-sick souls. They are pushing through the
crowd too.

You can push through. Go to Him. Respond to Him. Look to the one with fire in
His eyes. His eyes burn with love and passion for you.
Look to those eyes. Listen for that voice. Respond to that Man.
He is calling you out of the crowd. He is calling you to Himself.

NOW SET THE ATTENTION OF YOUR HEART ON THE LORD.
RECEIVE THE LOVE OF JESUS
AND LOVE HIM IN RETURN.

_____

_____

_____

_____

_____

_____

_____

_____

_____

_____

_____

_____

_____

_____

_____

_____

_____

_____

_____

_____

_____

_____

_____

_____

_____

_____

_____

_____

JOURNAL

# DAY 18

**"AND YOU WILL SEEK ME AND FIND ME, WHEN YOU SEARCH FOR ME WITH ALL YOUR HEART. I WILL BE FOUND BY YOU..."**
| JEREMIAH 29:13-14 |

---

It's the treasure of knowing God. It's the treasure of face to face and heart to heart exchange. It's the promise that if you draw near, that you will find Him.

"I will be found by you."

But there is a searching. There is a seeking. There is a journey. There is a pilgrimage.
Yes, a pilgrimage indeed.

It is a holy journey into the heart of the divine. A journey done in secret. A journey done in solitude. A journey through distraction. A journey through form devoid of power, religion without Presence. It's a journey and the prize and goal of it all is Him. Himself. All of Him. All of Him for all of you. In all these things He beckons and calls:

"Search for Me! Seek Me!"
With promise...
"You will find Me. I will be found by you!"

He invites the heart to journey into Him. Deeper. Further. His Presence cascading over you like an ever flowing waterfall of love. Even now, He calls again: "Give me everything. Give me ALL YOUR HEART."

Oh how He burns with passion for you! Burn with passion for Him! Let Him set you ablaze with passion and desire for Jesus! He has promised. He has pledged. You will find Him.

Go to Him. Seek Him. Give Him time. There is no cost that is too much!
Give all to get all in return. Let Him mark you in this place of seeking and finding and find the greatest treasure any man can ever find: The knowledge of God.

NOW SET THE ATTENTION OF YOUR HEART ON THE LORD.
RECEIVE THE LOVE OF JESUS
AND LOVE HIM IN RETURN.

_____
_____
_____
_____
_____
_____
_____
_____
_____
_____
_____
_____
_____
_____
_____
_____
_____
_____
_____
_____
_____
_____
_____
_____
_____

# JOURNAL

# DAY 19

**"YES INDEED I ALSO COUNT ALL THINGS LOSS FOR THE EXCELLENCE OF THE KNOWLEDGE OF CHRIST JESUS MY LORD... THAT I MAY KNOW HIM."**
| PHILIPPIANS 3:8,10 |

---

The Apostle Paul wrote of his secret. It was his motivation. It was his aim. He was an evangelist, a church planter, a spiritual father, and a builder and architect of the church that we now stand in and enjoy.

But he had a secret. He wasn't motivated by all of those things. Not really anyways. He had an aim. He had a goal. Everything that he did and everything that he was came back to this "one thing". What was his highest goal, greatest aim and biggest desire?

"That I may know Him."

Not know about Him. No. Something much more personal and much more intimate. Something that involved hearts colliding and souls merging. Something that spurs on the hungry heart and can only be satisfied by real and lasting spiritual exchange.

He desired to know Christ. For Himself. To know His Presence. To know His Person.

It's His Presence in the Secret Place of His Presence that changes and transforms. It's His Presence that sets our hearts ablaze and begins to burn the image of the One who formed us onto our hearts.

It's not performance. It's not religious "notches on a belt". It's not pedigrees and pomp. It's. Just. Jesus.

Knowing Him. Being known by Him. It's being still and being transformed. It's the cry of the Apostle Paul and it's the cry of your heart today. That you would know God and be known by God.
So know Him. Let Him be known by you. Go to Him again. Invite Him to come and touch you again. There is more.

NOW SET THE ATTENTION OF YOUR HEART ON THE LORD.
RECEIVE THE LOVE OF JESUS
AND LOVE HIM IN RETURN.

# JOURNAL

# DAY 20

"NOW IT HAPPENED AS THEY WENT THAT HE ENTERED A CERTAIN VILLAGE; AND A CERTAIN WOMAN NAMED MARTHA WELCOMED HIM INTO HER HOUSE. AND SHE HAD A SISTER CALLED MARY, WHO ALSO SAT AT JESUS' FEET AND HEARD HIS WORD. BUT MARTHA WAS DISTRACTED WITH MUCH SERVING, AND SHE APPROACHED HIM AND SAID, 'LORD, DO YOU NOT CARE THAT MY SISTER HAS LEFT ME TO SERVE ALONE? THEREFORE TELL HER TO HELP ME.' AND JESUS ANSWERED AND SAID TO HER, 'MARTHA, MARTHA, YOU ARE WORRIED AND TROUBLED ABOUT MANY THINGS. BUT ONE THING IS NEEDED, AND MARY HAS CHOSEN THAT GOOD PART, WHICH WILL NOT BE TAKEN AWAY FROM HER.'"

| LUKE 10:38-42 |

---

Are you distracted? Have you become preoccupied? It can happen to all of us. We can abandon the place of intimacy for the place of service.
No they are not mutually exclusive. Our love for God springs forth the fruit of service, sacrifice, and devotion.

But when Jesus walks into the room...

When Jesus walks into the room it's time to focus. It's time to be still. It's time to get low. It's time to listen.
It's time to be still and know... To know that He is God. To know that He is love. To know that He is calling us to Himself. To know that He holds the whole world in His hands.

He holds our dreams. He holds our fears. He holds our plans. He holds our regrets. He holds our efforts and He holds our weakness.
And in all these things... He. Is. God.
He is God and He has declared: One thing is necessary.

And what is that one thing? To be with Him. To be near Him. To sit at His feet and to listen for His voice. Mary saw her opportunity that day. She ignored the distractions and dialed into the Person. She drew near. She entered into a secret place while others hurriedly rushed around.

Jesus is with you now. Won't you draw near? Won't you get low? Won't you listen for His voice? He looks to you. He speaks: This love, this communion, this intimacy will not be taken away.

NOW SET THE ATTENTION OF YOUR HEART ON THE LORD.
RECEIVE THE LOVE OF JESUS
AND LOVE HIM IN RETURN.

_____
_____
_____
_____
_____
_____
_____
_____
_____
_____
_____
_____
_____
_____
_____
_____
_____
_____
_____
_____
_____
_____
_____
_____
_____
_____
_____
_____
_____
_____

# JOURNAL

# DAY 21

"AND THE ANGEL ANSWERED AND SAID TO HER, 'THE HOLY SPIRIT WILL COME UPON YOU, AND THE POWER OF THE HIGHEST WILL OVERSHADOW YOU; THEREFORE, ALSO, THAT HOLY ONE WHO IS TO BE BORN WILL BE CALLED THE SON OF GOD... FOR WITH GOD NOTHING WILL BE IMPOSSIBLE.'"
| LUKE 1:35, 37 |

---

And the Holy Spirit comes upon you. He covers you. He overshadows you. He draws you to a secret place and then visits you.

What happens in that place? What happens in the place where God touches man? What happens in that place where Holiness collides with humanity? What happens in that place when one heart, one soul responds and says "yes" to God? What happens in that place?

What happens in the place of shared love? What happens in that place of divinity crashing into the heart and mind of a surrendered soul?

The answer: Whatever God wants.

For nothing is impossible with God. He is God and He is here. He desires to overshadow you. He desires to deposit His very Person inside of your soul that you might release God in the earth.

What happens when you draw near? What happens when you say "yes"? What happens when time is given? Time? Yes! Time! Time to stay. Time to listen. Time to gaze. Time to ponder. Time to receive.

God is overshadowing you with Presence. Presence, yes, but power too! Such power! The same power that heals the sick. The same power that raises the dead. The same power that opens blind eyes and causes the deaf to hear and the lame to walk.

Here, in the secret place, He is wrapping you, covering you, overshadowing you with the power of the age to come. You are chosen. You are desired. God Himself has come... And in this place of communion, anything is possible.

NOW SET THE ATTENTION OF YOUR HEART ON THE LORD.
RECEIVE THE LOVE OF JESUS
AND LOVE HIM IN RETURN.

_____
_____
_____
_____
_____
_____
_____
_____
_____
_____
_____
_____
_____
_____
_____
_____
_____
_____
_____
_____
_____
_____
_____
_____
_____
_____
_____
_____
_____

# JOURNAL

# DAY 22

"THE NEXT DAY, AS THEY WENT ON THEIR JOURNEY AND DREW NEAR THE CITY, PETER WENT UP ON THE HOUSETOP TO PRAY, ABOUT THE SIXTH HOUR. THEN HE BECAME HUNGRY AND WANTED TO EAT; BUT WHILE THEY MADE READY, HE FELL INTO A TRANCE AND SAW HEAVEN OPENED AND AN OBJECT LIKE A GREAT SHEET BOUND AT THE FOUR CORNERS, DESCENDING TO HIM AND LET DOWN TO EARTH."
| ACTS 10:9-11 |

---

God! You visited Peter in the place of prayer. Lord, you opened his eyes and gave him revelation. You pulled back the veil of human wisdom and human understanding and you showed him realities of the spirit realm.

Lord, he sought you and you responded. You promised that you would come to us. You promised that when we came to You, You would come to us.

O God! Open my eyes today! Open my eyes today! Open my eyes! Soften my heart... here and now O God.

Lord, I want a greater revelation of Jesus Christ. I desire that the eyes of my heart would be opened... that my spirit would receive wisdom and revelation straight from Heaven.

God help me today. Help me press through to You.
Lord, in this place of prayer and in this place of connection, help me hear the words that you are speaking. Help my heart receive the revelation that you desire to share with me.

You said that you would pour out Your Spirit on the earth. You said You would send forth dreams, visions... prophetic revelation. God I am here and I am listening.

You visited Peter, now O God, visit me. Give me a heart to listen and obey. Give me a heart to press in and to hear something I have never heard before. Give me humility that I might receive the words of God and see them come to pass in my life. All I want is to know you more. I love everything that you do. Please open up the wells of revelation here in our secret place.

NOW SET THE ATTENTION OF YOUR HEART ON THE LORD.
RECEIVE THE LOVE OF JESUS
AND LOVE HIM IN RETURN.

_____
_____
_____
_____
_____
_____
_____
_____
_____
_____
_____
_____
_____
_____
_____
_____
_____
_____
_____
_____
_____
_____
_____
_____
_____

# JOURNAL

# DAY 23

"...THE LORD HAD CLOSED (HANNAH'S) WOMB... THEN SHE MADE A VOW AND SAID, 'O LORD OF HOSTS, IF YOU WILL INDEED LOOK ON THE AFFLICTION OF YOUR MAIDSERVANT AND REMEMBER ME, AND NOT FORGET YOUR MIADSERVANT, BUT WILL GIVE YOUR MAIDSERVANT A MALE CHILD, THEN I WILL GIVE HIM TO THE LORD... SO IT CAME TO PASS IN THE PROCESS OF TIME THAT HANNAH CONCEIVED AND BORE A SON, AND CALLED HIS NAME SAMUEL, SAYING, 'BECAUSE I HAVE ASKED FOR HIM FROM THE LORD.'"
| 1 SAMUEL 1:6, 11, 20 |

---

The Secret Place of His Presence isn't only for communion. It isn't only for intimacy. It isn't only for revelation. It is also the place of petition. It is the place of coming before the Lord, to ask for His hand to move in our lives.

It is the place of boldly coming before the throne of grace. It is the place where the scepter is lowered and we approach the King of Glory, the Ruler of the Universe. All power is His and He does what He pleases. Who could possibly contest with God?!

And yet there is a place of influence. There is a place of friendship. There is a place where our thoughts matter. Our desires matter. There is a place where we come to God in light of how things currently are, and we speak to God where things need to change.

We bring our pain, our hopes, our dreams, our desires, our needs, our concerns... We bring it all. We bring it all to God and we appeal to God for change.

We do not beg as those devoid of relationship. We come as the beloved of God. We come in the Beloved of God. Even as Jesus Christ the Righteous stands at the right hand of God the Father and lives to make intercession for us, we join in that intercession and petition the Father to stretch forth His hand in our lives.

What troubles you today? Take it before Him. Take it now... to the Secret Place of His Presence and lift your voice before Him. Jesus has prepared this place for you. Run in. Lift your voice. Petition a faithful God and then watch Him move mightily in your life.

NOW SET THE ATTENTION OF YOUR HEART ON THE LORD.
RECEIVE THE LOVE OF JESUS
AND LOVE HIM IN RETURN.

_____
_____
_____
_____
_____
_____
_____
_____
_____
_____
_____
_____
_____
_____
_____
_____
_____
_____
_____
_____
_____
_____
_____
_____
_____
_____
_____
_____
_____
_____
_____

# JOURNAL

# DAY 24

"AND THIS IS ETERNAL LIFE, THAT THEY MAY KNOW YOU, THE ONLY TRUE GOD, AND JESUS CHRIST WHOM YOU HAVE SENT."
| JOHN 17:3 |

---

Jesus Christ, the Author and Perfecter of our faith... Our Savior, Healer, and Deliverer... The Provider of our Salvation and the initiator of eternal life defined it for us in the Gospel of John.

What is eternal life? It is knowing God. It is knowing God the Father and God the Son. It is Union with Him in the Presence of the Holy Spirit. It is being joined to the author and giver of life.

This is eternal life.

Today, wherever you are... whatever your week has looked like or how you felt before you began reading... Eternity is crashing into your temporal. The Ancient of Days... The Father... The Lord of Glory... He is making Himself known to you even right now.

His Presence is invading your life. His Glory is washing over your heart and mind. His power is surging through your being and in so doing He is conforming you to His image and to His likeness.

For it is in knowing Him that we are changed.
Here in the secret place there is time and space for Him to move. Here in the secret place He is the goal and He is the aim. He is the desire and He is the point.

Not merely knowing about Him, but knowing Him personally, intimately. Knowing the Father and knowing the Son. Face to face. Heart to heart. Eternal Life? Yes! Eternal life that begins today and stretches forth with no end. And suddenly I realize this is my calling for all of eternity.
I will spend eternity future plumbing the depths of the knowledge of God. But today, in the secret place, I take another step in the journey.

God, I. Want. To. Know. You.

NOW SET THE ATTENTION OF YOUR HEART ON THE LORD.
RECEIVE THE LOVE OF JESUS
AND LOVE HIM IN RETURN.

# JOURNAL

# DAY 25

**"DRAW NEAR TO GOD AND HE WILL DRAW NEAR TO YOU."**
| JAMES 4:8 |

---

I'm alive because you called my name. I was dead in the tomb. I was unable to move in your direction. I was in sin. I was ashamed. I was lost. I was broken.

But you spoke. You called me by name. My heart began to beat and I became alive. Yes, You called me by name.

You gave me grace. Your grace is teaching me, leading me, guiding me. Your grace is changing me. Your grace calls me near.

Today you say, "Draw near to me and I will draw near to you."

I used to be bound. I used to be paralyzed. I was unable to move towards you. But you made me alive. So today, I move in Your direction. I move towards You.

God you said for me to make the first move. So I'm moving! I'm drawing near. I'm leaning in, pressing in, searching and seeking. I am not content with what I know and I can't eat yesterday's bread. I need to encounter you today I and I need a fresh revelation of Jesus Christ.

So I am drawing near. I'm setting aside time. I'm making space. I'm searching Your Word and I'm hosting Your Presence. I want to be known by God and I want to lean in your direction.

God you said if I leaned into you that you would respond! God! Here I am God! I'm coming in Your direction! Now O God, come in mine! Jesus! I'm crying out to You today! Remember Your Word O God. My greatest reward in life is simply to know You more.

So today, I draw near. I draw near and I look to You to draw near to me. Come to me God. Reveal Yourself. My heart burns for Jesus. I must know you more.

NOW SET THE ATTENTION OF YOUR HEART ON THE LORD.
RECEIVE THE LOVE OF JESUS
AND LOVE HIM IN RETURN.

_____
_____
_____
_____
_____
_____
_____
_____
_____
_____
_____
_____
_____
_____
_____
_____
_____
_____
_____
_____
_____
_____
_____
_____
_____

# JOURNAL

# DAY 26

**"FOR HE WHO IS JOINED TO THE LORD IS ONE SPIRIT WITH HIM."**
| 1 CORINTHIANS 6:17 |

---

Lord.
My God.

What can I say?

You have joined Yourself to me.

So much deeper than forgiveness. My sins? Yes they have been forgiven.
My future? Yes it is secure. My present? My present is His Presence. Beyond
forgiveness. Beyond reconciliation. I enter into the doors of Union. He has
joined Himself to me.

I'm not the same. Something has changed. I am not the same substance and
I am not the same creature. I've been made new. I've been born again. I have
become a new creation.

The seed? The seed is the very Word of God Himself. He has joined Himself to
me.

These things are too great and marvelous for me. I shudder when I think...
I worship... I bow. I am quieted and I am still. Before Your Glory... Before the
Glory of what you have done in me and to me. I am changed because you
have drawn near.

So I step again into the Union. I turn my attention to the Union. You have
joined Yourself to me.

God I ask that wave after wave of Your Glory Presence would flood my heart.
I ask for deepening revelations of the goodness of God and the nearness of
God and the beauty of God.

Here in our secret place, I turn my attention to you again. I lift my gaze again. I
ask for more again. Having been filled, I am all the more hungry. Having been
satisfied, I thirst all the more. Jesus. You. Are. My. Everything.

51

NOW SET THE ATTENTION OF YOUR HEART ON THE LORD.
RECEIVE THE LOVE OF JESUS
AND LOVE HIM IN RETURN.

_____
_____
_____
_____
_____
_____
_____
_____
_____
_____
_____
_____
_____
_____
_____
_____
_____
_____
_____
_____
_____
_____
_____
_____
_____
_____
_____
_____
_____
_____

# JOURNAL

# DAY 27

"BEHOLD WHAT MANNER OF LOVE THE FATHER HAS BESTOWED ON US, THAT WE SHOULD
BE CALLED CHILDREN OF GOD! ...BELOVED, NOW WE ARE CHILDREN OF GOD; AND IT HAS NOT
YET BEEN REVEALED WHAT WE SHALL BE, BUT WE KNOW THAT WHEN HE IS REVEALED, WE
SHALL BE LIKE HIM, FOR WE SHALL SEE HIM AS HE IS."
| 1 JOHN 3:1-2 |

---

God I've come today to wonder. I've come today to ponder. I've come today to
consider what you have done in me and what is to come. I've come to a quiet
place... a place of my soul resting in the fact that I am family with God. Yes, I.
Am. Family.

He is my Father. I am Your Child. I am Your offspring. I bear Your name. Your
blood flows through my veins.

I am Your Family.

And yet... there is a day. O yes, there is a day.

There is a day when I will see you fully. I will know you fully. I will see you for
Who You are. On that day, I will be changed. I don't know it all. I don't know
much. But I know that I will be like you when I see You.

O God! Just to see You! This is the desire of my soul! To know you, to see You.
To know You and to be known by You! I want to be known by God.

Lord as I rest here in Your Presence. As Your Spirit testifies to the truth of
Your Word, my heart anchors in Your love. It was Your awesome love that led
You to the cross. It was Your awesome love that led You to seek me, to save
me. So I am here.

You drew me to Yourself and now I am here. I know you and I am known by
You. But one day, I will be fully known.

How close can I get on this side of eternity?
How much can I see today?
I don't know the limits, but I want to find out.
Take me to depths. You have my heart. I am Yours.

NOW SET THE ATTENTION OF YOUR HEART ON THE LORD.
RECEIVE THE LOVE OF JESUS
AND LOVE HIM IN RETURN.

_____
_____
_____
_____
_____
_____
_____
_____
_____
_____
_____
_____
_____
_____
_____
_____
_____
_____
_____
_____
_____
_____
_____
_____
_____
_____
_____

# JOURNAL

# DAY 28

"...BUT AS HE WENT, THE MULTITUDES THRONGED HIM. NOW A WOMAN, HAVING A FLOW OF BLOOD FOR TWELVE YEARS, WHO HAD SPENT ALL HER LIVELIHOOD ON PHYSICIANS AND COULD NOT BE HEALED BY ANY, CAME FROM BEHIND AND TOUCHED THE BORDER OF HIS GARMENT. AND IMMEDIATELY HER FLOW OF BLOOD STOPPED."
| LUKE 8:42-44 |

---

There was a crowd. There was distraction. There was a Savior. There was a need. There was hunger. There was desperation. There was a determination that would refuse to be denied. There was a woman who laid hold of something that no one else knew was possible.

And there, in a crowd, she found a secret place.

She accessed the Savior. She accessed the Healer. She touched Eternity and Eternity touched her.

In that moment her faith caused her to reach, to stretch, to push through and press in... Until. She. Touched. God.

Oh! That I would have a heart like that! Oh! That I would touch God! Even today! How I want to touch God! I desire to touch eternity! I desire to press through my distractions... And the voices! The voices that mock me and discourage me.

The voices that say, "There is no hope in God for him!"

Today, I refuse to listen to the voice of discouragement. I refuse to listen to the voice of past experience. I know the Savior is within reach. So I will reach out.

Just a touch.

Just the fringe.

Just the edge of His garment.
I will touch God today. This is MY secret place.

NOW SET THE ATTENTION OF YOUR HEART ON THE LORD.
RECEIVE THE LOVE OF JESUS
AND LOVE HIM IN RETURN.

_____
_____
_____
_____
_____
_____
_____
_____
_____
_____
_____
_____
_____
_____
_____
_____
_____
_____
_____
_____
_____
_____
_____
_____
_____
_____
_____
_____
_____

# JOURNAL

# DAY 29

"AFTER THESE THINGS I LOOKED, AND BEHOLD, A DOOR STANDING OPEN IN HEAVEN. AND THE FIRST VOICE WHICH I HEARD WAS LIKE A TRUMPET SPEAKING WITH ME, SAYING, "COME UP HERE, AND I WILL SHOW YOU THINGS WHICH MUST TAKE PLACE AFTER THIS."
| REVELATION 4:1 |

---

And there is a door. You have appointed a door standing open for me. You have opened the vault, the treasury of heaven. You have made a way and today in the secret place You call me.

I hear the voice to come up. I hear the voice to come closer. I hear the voice that is calling me home... calling me close.

I hear the voice calling me. For today you desire to share Your heart with me. Today You desire to show me things I have never seen before. You call me not just to knowledge but to intimacy. You desire to show me things for You love me. You have set Your affection upon me. You desire to share things with me heart to heart.

So I walk through the door. Those who do not go through the door are thieves and robbers. But not me. I am Your friend and I am Your beloved. I know the Door, for You are the Door.

You are my access to the Father in the Spirit. You, Yourself. You have become to me a doorway to intimacy with the Father.

Jesus Christ I worship you today. I long for you today. I want and I desire for you to take up residence in me... in my heart... in my soul... in my mind.

Be enthroned in me.

Be glorified in me.

I draw near to you in the secret place. I respond to the voice. I walk through the door. Be glorified in me.

NOW SET THE ATTENTION OF YOUR HEART ON THE LORD.
RECEIVE THE LOVE OF JESUS
AND LOVE HIM IN RETURN.

_____
_____
_____
_____
_____
_____
_____
_____
_____
_____
_____
_____
_____
_____
_____
_____
_____
_____
_____
_____
_____
_____
_____
_____
_____
_____
_____
_____
_____

# JOURNAL

# DAY 30

"AND THE SPIRIT AND THE BRIDE SAY, 'COME!' AND LET HIM WHO HEARS SAY, 'COME!'
AND LET HIM WHO THIRSTS COME. WHOEVER DESIRES, LET HIM TAKE THE WATER OF LIFE
FREELY... EVEN SO, COME, LORD JESUS!"
| REVELATION 22:17, 20 |

---

It comes to this. It has always been this. A heart that thirsts. A soul that desires. It's a hunger that isn't of my own making. You have put it in me. You have caused me to hunger. You have caused me to thirst.

My greatest desire and my highest aim is to know you. To be near you. To see You. To hear You.

I join with the Spirit. I join in with the bride. I join in with the hungry and the thirsty.

Come Lord.

Come.

We desire you above wealth.

We desire you above fame.

We desire you above all.

All we want is you. To know You. To see You. To be known by You.

Come.

Come Lord Jesus.

In all Your glory. In all Your splendor. In all Your majesty. In all Your wonder.

Please kindle fresh love for Jesus in me Holy Spirit. That He would have first place here, now, in this moment, and forever.
This. Is. My. Secret Place.

NOW SET THE ATTENTION OF YOUR HEART ON THE LORD.
RECEIVE THE LOVE OF JESUS
AND LOVE HIM IN RETURN.

_____
_____
_____
_____
_____
_____
_____
_____
_____
_____
_____
_____
_____
_____
_____
_____
_____
_____
_____
_____
_____
_____
_____
_____
_____
_____
_____

# JOURNAL

# DAY 1

"As the deer pants for the water brooks, so pants my soul for You, O God. My soul thirsts for God, for the living God. When shall I come and appear before God?"
| PSALM 42:1-2 |

# DAY 2

He who dwells in the secret place of the Most High shall abide under the shadow of the Almighty."
| PSALM 91:1 |

# DAY 3

"LORD, You have been our dwelling place in all generations."
| PSALM 90:1 |

# DAY 4

"One thing I have desired of the LORD, that will I seek: That I may dwell in the house of the LORD all the days of my life, to behold the beauty of the LORD, and to inquire in His temple. For in the time of trouble He shall hide me in His pavilion: In the secret place of His tabernacle He shall hide me: He shall set me high upon a rock."
| PSALM 27:4-5 |

# DAY 5

"Then [Moses] said to Him, 'If Your Presence does not go with us, do not bring us up from here.'"
| EXODUS 33:15 |

# DAY 6

"And [Moses] said, 'Please, show me Your glory.' Then He said, "I will make all my goodness pass before you, and I will proclaim the name of the LORD before you.'"
| EXODUS 33:18-19 |

# DAY 7

"And the LORD said, 'Shall I hide from Abraham what I am doing?'"
| GENESIS 18:17 |

# DAY 8

And God said, 'Let Us make man in Our image, according to our likeness.'"
| GENESIS 1:26 |

# DAY 9

"Then [Jacob] dreamed, and behold, a ladder was set up on the earth, and its top reached to heaven; and there the angels of God were ascending and descending on it."
| GENESIS 28:12 |

# DAY 10

"So the LORD spoke to Moses face to face, as a man speaks to his friend. And he would return to the camp, but his servant Joshua the son of Nun, a young man, did not depart from the tabernacle." | EXODUS 33:11 |

# DAY 11

"...I saw the Lord sitting on a throne, high and lifted up, and the train of His robe filled the temple. Above it stood seraphim... and one cried to another and said: 'Holy, holy, holy is the LORD of hosts; The whole earth is full of His glory!' And the posts of the door were shaken by the voice of him who cried out, and the house was filled with smoke."
| ISAIAH 6:1-4 |

# DAY 12

"Heaven is My throne, and earth is My footstool. Where is the house that you will build Me? And where is the place of My rest? ...But on this one will I look: On him who is poor and of a contrite sprit, and who trembles at My word."
| ISAIAH 66:1-2 |

# DAY 13

So let us know, let us press on to know the LORD. His going forth is as certain as the dawn; And He will come to us like the rain, Like the spring rain watering the earth."
| HOSEA 6:3 NASB |

# DAY 14

"He bowed the heavens also, and came down with darkness under His feet. And He rode upon a cherub, and flew; He flew upon the wings of the wind. He made darkness His secret place..." | PSALM 18:9-11 |

# DAY 15

"O my dove, in the clefts of the rock,
in the secret places of the cliff,
Let me see your face,
Let me hear your voice;
For your voice is sweet,
And your face is lovely."
| SONG OF SOLOMON 2:14 |

# DAY 16

"But you, when you pray, go into your room,
and when you have shut your door,
pray to your Father who is in the secret place;
and your Father who sees in secret will reward you openly."
| MATTHEW 6:6 |

# DAY 17

"And He went up on the mountain and called to Him those
He Himself wanted. And they came to Him."
| MARK 3:13 |

# DAY 18

"And you will seek Me and find Me,
when you search for Me with all your heart.
I will be found by you…"
| JEREMIAH 29:13-14 |

# DAY 19

"Yes indeed I also count all things loss for the excellence of
the knowledge of Christ Jesus my Lord… that I may know
Him."
| PHILIPPIANS 3:8,10 |

# DAY 20

"Now it happened as they went that He entered a certain
village; and a certain woman named Martha welcomed
Him into her house. And she had a sister called Mary, who
also sat at Jesus' feet and heard His word. But Martha was
distracted with much serving, and she approached Him
and said, 'Lord, do You not care that my sister has left me
to serve alone? Therefore tell her to help me.' And Jesus
answered and said to her, 'Martha, Martha, you are worried
and troubled about many things. But one thing is needed,
and Mary has chosen that good part, which will not be taken
away from her.'" | LUKE 10:38-42 |

# DAY 21

"And the angel answered and said to her, 'The Holy Spirit will come upon you, and the power of the Highest will overshadow you; therefore, also, that Holy One who is to be born will be called the Son of God... For with God nothing will be impossible.'"
| LUKE 1:35, 37 |

# DAY 22

"The next day, as they went on their journey and drew near the city, Peter went up on the housetop to pray, about the sixth hour. Then he became hungry and wanted to eat; but while they made ready, he fell into a trance and saw heaven opened and an object like a great sheet bound at the four corners, descending to him and let down to earth."
| ACTS 10:9-11 |

# DAY 23

"...the Lord had closed [Hannah's] womb... Then she made a vow and said, 'O LORD of hosts, if You will indeed look on the affliction of Your maidservant and remember me, and not forget Your miadservant, but will give Your maidservant a male child, then I will give him to the LORD... So it cam to pass in the process of time that Hannah conceived and bore a son, and called his name Samuel, saying, 'Because I have asked for him from the LORD.'"
| ACTS 10:9-11 |

# DAY 24

**"And this is eternal life, that they may know You, the only true God, and Jesus Christ whom You have sent."**
| JOHN 17:3 |

# DAY 25

**"Draw near to God and He will draw near to you."**
| JAMES 4:8 |

# DAY 26

**"For he who is joined to the Lord is one spirit with Him"**
| 1 CORINTHIANS 6:17 |

# DAY 27

**"Behold what manner of love the Father has bestowed on us, that we should be called children of God! ...Beloved, now we are children of God; and it has not yet been revealed what we shall be, but we know that when He is revealed, we shall be like Him, for we shall see Him as He is."**
| 1 JOHN 3:1-2 |

# DAY 28

"…But as He went, the multitudes thronged Him. Now a woman, having a flow of blood for twelve years, who had spent all her livelihood on physicians and could not be healed by any, came from behind and touched the border of His garment. And immediately her flow of blood stopped."
| LUKE 8:42-44 |

# DAY 29

"After these things I looked, and behold, a door standing open in heaven. And the first voice which I heard was like a trumpet speaking with me, saying, "Come up here, and I will show you things which must take place after this."
| REVELATION 4:1 |

# DAY 30

"And the Spirit and the bride say, 'Come!' And let him who hears say, 'Come!' And let him who thirsts come. Whoever desires, let him take the water of life freely… Even so, come, Lord Jesus!"
| REVELATION 22:17, 20 |

# Liked it? Loved it?

PLEASE LEAVE A REVIEW ON
AMAZON.COM

Elani
PUBLISHING

www.ingramcontent.com/pod-product-compliance
Lightning Source LLC
LaVergne TN
LVHW091232080426
835509LV00009B/1245